SERVICE
LEARNING

Volunteering to Help with Animals

Claudia Isler

HIGH
interest
books

Children's Press
A Division of Grolier Publishing
New York / London / Hong Kong / Sydney
Danbury, Connecticut

For Phoebe, one amazing cat

Contributing Editor: Rob Kirkpatrick
Book Design: Michael DeLisio

Photo Credits: Cover, p. 6, 11, 19 © Indexstock; p. 4, 16, 28, 34, 38, 41 © International Stock; p. 9, 31 © Image Bank; p. 12, 32 by Maura Boruchow; p. 15 by Nelson Sa; p. 20 © AP Wide World Photos; p. 23, 24, 37 © Corbis.

Visit Children's Press on the Internet at:
http://publishing.grolier.com

Library of Congress Cataloging-in-Publication Data

Isler, Claudia.
    Volunteering to help animals / by Claudia Isler.
        p. cm. – (Service learning)
    Includes bibliographical references and index.
    ISBN 0-516-23397-1 (lib. bdg.) – ISBN 0-516-23575-3 (pbk.)
    1. Child volunteers—United States—Juvenile literature. 2. Young volunteers—United States—Juvenile literature. 3. Animal welfare—United States—Juvenile literature. 4. Animal rescue—United States—Juvenile literature. [1. Voluntarism. 2. Animals—Treatment.] I. Title. II. Series.

HQ784.V64 I75 2000
361.3'7—dc21

                                                                00-029520

CONTENTS

INTRODUCTION

Many people hunt and kill animals for food. We use animal skins to make clothing, shoes, bags, and blankets. We also turn animals into pets.

Some people abuse animals because they think it is fun. Others damage the animals' habitats (where animals live in nature). Because of these problems, animals need our help.

Throughout the world, many people work to save animals' natural habitats. Other people study animals in zoos to better understand how they behave and what they need to survive. At rescue centers and animal shelters, people help birds, dogs, cats, horses, and other animals that have been abused, injured, or orphaned.

Many jobs that help animals can be performed by service-learning volunteers (unpaid student workers). All you need to get started is time, patience, willingness, and a love of animals.

This service learner is enjoying her work with a calf.

CHAPTER ONE

WHAT IS SERVICE LEARNING?

Service learning is an opportunity offered by many schools or community organizations. Service-learning projects help you to get involved in your community through volunteer service. Volunteers who take part in service learning are students. They become service learners to become more aware of the world outside of the classroom. Then they use their experiences as service learners in other areas of life.

Service-learning projects can give you the chance to build skills you'll need in school. These skills can help get you into college or help you find a great job. Many schools require that their students complete some

Service learning can add an exciting new aspect to school.

volunteer service to graduate. Even your school does not have a service-learning requirement, you still can learn a lot from volunteering.

HOW SERVICE LEARNING WORKS

Service-learning work can be done either through organizations or on an individual basis. Service groups and individual service learners work on projects to help their community. They get together with an adviser and plan a community project. They decide what their goals are and what they will need to reach these goals. After the project, they talk about whether they met their goals, which parts of the plan worked, and which parts didn't.

WHAT YOUR PROJECT
CAN DO FOR ANIMALS

You can help animals in so many ways. Dogs and cats at shelters need people to play with

Caring for animals can be a fun service-learning project.

them. They need people to pet them, feed them, clean their cages, and walk them. Zoos and aquariums often are looking for volunteers. Wild animals sometimes need help, too. Some get hurt and need medical attention. After they heal, they need to be trained to survive on their own in the wild. This is called rehabilitation.

Animals are an important part of life on our planet. The areas in which they live deserve to be protected by people. You can help animals by helping to conserve their natural habitats, too.

WHAT SERVICE LEARNING CAN DO FOR YOU

Service learning may help you to organize ideas and budget your time. These skills can help you a lot in school. You also can benefit in other ways from service-learning work.

FAST FACT

Seagulls in seaside communities look everywhere for food. Volunteers in Santa Barbara, California, had to clean some gulls very carefully with dish soap after the birds got into an uncovered grease pit behind a restaurant.

School Credit

Many schools require that you complete a service-learning project before you graduate. If your school does not have this requirement, you still might be able to arrange to do service learning for independent study. Ask

Service learning lets students work with each other.

your guidance counselor or favorite teacher about this opportunity.

If you do a service-learning project through school, you might have to write a paper about the work you've done. Or you might have to give a presentation. This is your chance to tell other people what you did and what you learned.

Applying to Colleges

Many colleges and universities are interested in more than your grades or SAT (Scholastic

You will be able to describe your service-learning experiences when you apply to colleges.

Aptitude Test) scores. The admissions staff likes to see young people who have become involved in causes. Helping your community looks good on applications. Many applications require students to write personal essays. When you write your essay, you can explain your service-learning experience. Your service experience will show that you will be an active and helpful member of your college community.

Getting a Job

Just as college admissions officers are impressed by service-learning experience, so are many employers. In fact, a lot of large companies encourage their employees to do service learning. That's because service-learning skills are useful in the workplace. Leadership, organizational skills, and public speaking are just a few of the work skills you develop from your service project. You also will gain experience in getting along with many different types of people.

DID YOU KNOW?

The Corporation for National Service awards President's Student Service Scholarships. One junior and one senior from each high school in the country can apply for a $1,000 scholarship. Kids ages five to fourteen who perform 50 hours of community service within a one-year period can receive a silver pin with the presidential seal. They also get a certificate and a letter from the president.

Serve and Research

A big part of service learning is discussing what your service work has taught you. For example, in Lewisburg, Pennsylvania, the high school offers a program called the Senior Service and Research Project. When the students are done with their project, they must evaluate it. They discuss whether they achieved their goals, and why they did or didn't. They discuss problems they encountered, how the project could be improved, and what they learned from it.

KEEPING A JOURNAL

When you're involved in service learning, you can work on many exciting projects. You should keep a journal for every project that you do. Your journal will help you to organize your thoughts if you have to give a presentation or write a research paper about your project. All the information you'll need will be at your fingertips.

Keep a journal to help you remember and evaluate your service work.

1. What animals did I work with today?

2. How did I help animals today?

3. Did I learn anything new today about animals?

4. Today was hard because _____ .

5. I felt really happy today because _____

6. What new people did I meet? What did I learn from them?

7. How is the work I did today related to my project?

CHAPTER TWO

ANIMALS ALL AROUND

Before you can get started, you have to think about what interests you. Is there a particular animal that you really like? Working with animals is demanding. How dirty do you want to get? What kinds of skills do you have to offer? It's also important not to be scared of the animals. If you'd like to help them but you're a little nervous about handling them, there are other ways you can help. You could clean and paint an animal shelter. You could update computer records for a vet or help raise funds for a zoo.

Once you know about what kind of work you're interested in, you need to think about

Are you a horse lover? You could find a
fun service-learning project on a farm.

all of the other things that might affect the job you do.

TIME

How much time do you have to give to your project? Are you available after school, before school, or only on the weekends? For a lot of jobs that involve working with animals, you will have to be there very early in the morning. For example, at the zoo you may have to get the animals ready in the morning for any visitors they might get during the day.

If you've decided on a project that requires more time than you have to give, you need to pick something else. If your project includes volunteering at an organization, the staff will expect you to be dependable. You will have to be there when you are scheduled. Think about your homework, household chores, and other extracurricular (outside of class) activities that you need to do and budget your time accordingly.

As you plan your service-learning project, find out the places you need to go and how you will get there.

TRANSPORTATION

Where will you be working? How will you get there? Will you need to travel to different locations? Are you going to need a ride? Check with family members and anyone else who might be giving you a lift. You may have to work your schedule around theirs.

FUND-RAISING

Maybe you and some friends want to start your own project. For example, you could

*Working at an animal shelter can be
a great service-learning project.*

educate your community about the benefits of having their pets fixed (spayed or neutered). To do this, first you'll need to advertise what you're doing. Think about how you will pay for the supplies to make posters and flyers.

GETTING PERMISSION

Your family will want to know how much time you will be spending on your service-learning project. They'll want to know where you have to go, especially if someone has to drive you there. Your teacher may have to make arrangements for you to get an empty classroom for your project team's meetings. A store owner or manager may let you set up an information table. To get permission from all of these people, you will have to be very clear about what you plan to do and why. Write a statement that clearly describes your project.

PROJECT IDEAS

There are a lot of ways to help animals. You might consider some of the following ideas:

Gimme Shelter

Animal shelters usually house dogs and cats. These animals are there for many reasons. Some are abandoned and found as strays. Others have been rescued from owners who mistreated them. They may be the puppies and kittens of pets that were not fixed. There are a lot of jobs to do at shelters. You can walk dogs, clean cages, and feed the animals.

Some of these animals need to learn to feel safe again with people. You can be the first one they learn to trust! Puppies and kittens also need experience with people before they make great pets. You can teach a puppy not to jump all over you and knock you down whenever she sees you. You also might be able to do some office work at a shelter.

Wildlife Rescue

If you're interested in helping wild animals, you might try a wildlife center, such as the Hudson Valley Raptor Center in Stanfordville, New York, or the Santa Barbara Wildlife Care Network in Santa Barbara, California. Birds, such as owls and hawks, often are injured by people, sometimes by kids playing with BB guns. If they're lucky, these birds can be rehabilitated. Sometimes animals lose their mothers and cannot survive. A fawn whose mother is killed by a car will die unless someone feeds it and teaches it what it needs to

You could volunteer to work with owls and other animals at a wildlife center.

know to survive in the wild. Wildlife rescue organizations need volunteers to feed animals and clean out cages. Be sure to check with an organization about age requirements. Some places can't use workers under the age of 18.

Horses need a lot of care, such as taking care of their bridles and saddles.

HELPING ANIMALS HELPS PEOPLE

We've learned that animals can help people, too. Humans benefit from petting animals and receiving affection from animals. Studies have shown that people who have pets are happier and live longer than people without pets. Some programs bring nursing home residents together with pets. Playing with the animals helps to keep people healthy and happy. You can help take care of these animals and be a part of the program that brings them to the people who need them.

For example, you could work with seeing-eye dogs. You could help their owners with caring for and training them. Also, there are ranches and stables that help people with disabilities. They provide lessons in horseback riding to the physically or mentally

FAST FACT

Rescue workers saved five baby owls from their nest after their mother was killed. The volunteers had to feed the babies with a gloved hand. They covered the glove with feathers from the mother so the babies wouldn't think humans were their parents!

challenged. Horses need lots of care, but it's hard and dirty work, so be prepared. You can muck out (clean) stalls. You can feed and water the horses. You can groom them, or take care of the equipment that goes with riding, such as the bridles and saddles.

In New York City, many people worked with the parks department to clean up Turtle Pond. The water and the trees and grasses around it now are home to many kinds of birds, including ducks, herons, and swans. These birds fly into the heart of the city to build their nests! In rural areas, you may be able to combat land development that threatens the habitats of local wildlife. As long as animals have safe places to live and food to eat, they have a chance to survive.

FAST FACT

In Kentucky, Clay County high school students have created and maintained the Anakawi Nature Trail. The students test the water for pollution and test the health of plants and insects. They have created walking trails, a frog and turtle pond, a wildlife observatory, and much more.

CHAPTER THREE

WHO, WHAT, WHERE, WOOF

Do you know what kind of project you want to do? If you do, you need to work on getting your project together. Careful planning will help you to achieve your goal.

BUILD A TEAM

Working with others who share your interests can be a lot of fun. Try to find people with whom you'd like to approach the local animal shelter as a group. You can offer your services as a team. Lots of shelters would be thrilled to take on a group of volunteers to help care for the animals. You can hang up flyers to advertise for volunteers. You can ask for permission to set up a sign-up table in the

cafeteria at school. Or make an announcement about your plan at the start of class.

MISSION STATEMENT

One of the best ways to make sure that your team is clear on the plan is to write a mission statement. A mission statement is a document that explains what your goals are. It also explains how you plan to reach your goals. Here's an example:

"Pet Protectors is a volunteer organization devoted to educating the public about the benefits of fixing their pets. We believe that informing people of the health benefits to animals and the health and financial benefits to the community will be good for our town. It will improve the lives of pets and their owners. It also will help other residents, who will worry less about stray dogs and cats on their property. Volunteers will use their free time to hand out informative flyers and talk to the public in stores, malls, and their school."

Service learners can help others understand how best to care for animals.

FIND SPONSORS

What if you want to open an animal shelter in your community? That would take a lot of time. It also would take lots and lots of money. That's where sponsors come in. A sponsor is a person or an organization that pays for and some-times helps you to carry out a project. In some cases, people will take you more seriously if your pro-ject has a sponsor. Community members might be more willing to donate funds, equipment, or space.

FAST FACT

A fifth-grade class in Washington state raised $250 for their local humane society by selling home-made cookies door-to-door.

ADVERTISE

There are different ways to advertise. Think about who you're trying to reach and choose the method that will work best for your project.

PetWorld

Adopt-a-Puppy week

*You could make ads to promote
your service-learning project.*

Press Releases

A press release is a short notice (no more than one page) about your project that you can send to local TV stations, radio stations, and newspapers. They might even send a reporter to talk to you. Your press release should have a headline that is catchy but not misleading. It should include the name and

Contact your local radio or television station to see about running public service announcements (PSAs).

phone number of the person that people can call for more information. Your press release should say whose project it is, what the project is, when and where it will take place, and why you're doing it.

Public Service Announcements

Public service announcements (PSAs) are short statements that can be read on TV or on the radio. Many cable channels provide free airtime for this purpose. PSAs are only 10 to 30 seconds long. Give the name and address of your organization, the cause you are working for, and the name and phone number of the person to call for more information. Include the dates you want the PSA to start on the air and the date you want it off the air. Contact your local TV and radio stations to find out how to submit your PSA.

Posters and Flyers

One of the simplest ways to advertise is to make flyers and posters. These advertisements can be a great way to let people know about your project. Your ads can be put in store windows and on community bulletin boards in community centers, places of worship, and supermarkets. You can even hand out flyers on the street.

CHAPTER FOUR

PAWS AND REFLECT

An important part of service learning is understanding what your work taught you. As you do your service-learning work, pay attention to everything you do and everyone you meet. Afterward, think about how your work has changed you and your community.

NEW PEOPLE, NEW EXPERIENCES

When you build a team that is interested in achieving the same goals, you almost always meet new people. It's the same when you join any team or club at school. Your project team members may have valuable skills and ideas from which you can learn. Then, when your team heads for the local animal shelter, zoo,

Working with animals can help you to discover your natural abilities.

35

aquarium, or wildlife rescue station, you all will meet the professionals who have chosen this field as their career. You could meet veterinarians (doctors for animals), zoologists (scientists who classify animals), and marine biologists (scientists who study animals that live underwater).

Working with different animals can give you many new experiences. The volunteers who had to clean seagulls with dish soap had no prior experience in washing birds! Even teaching an abused dog to trust you can be exciting and new.

Shadowing Animals

At some zoos, volunteers are asked to shadow certain animals, such as seals. This means that the volunteer follows the animal around for the day. You take notes on things such as where it goes, and when and how much it eats. This helps the zoo to stay aware of the animal's health. It also gives scientists

At zoos and aquariums, service learners can volunteer to work with exotic animals.

important information about the habits of seals. Plus, it gives you a chance to learn all about seals, up close and in person.

EVALUATING YOUR PROJECT

The questions you've asked yourself while keeping a journal will help you to evaluate your project in several ways:

1. How did the community benefit from your work with animals?
2. How did you benefit from your work with animals?
3. How did you help animals?
4. Did you achieve your goal?

Answering these questions will help you to think about the work you've done. Did anything go wrong? What did you learn from any goals you were not able to achieve this time? If you understand what worked about your project and what didn't, you'll be prepared for any project on which you decide to work in the future.

After your project, ask yourself how you helped animals.

Looking Ahead

Maybe you thought about other possible projects while you were at work on this one. Now that you have some experience with animals, you can pursue these new goals. You can take classes that focus on your new interests, especially if you think you'd like a career in working with animals. You can join clubs or other organizations that share your interests. You can read many, many books on subjects that interest you. In helping animals, you have become an active member of your community. There's no reason to stop there!

Helping animals makes you an active member of your community!

extracurricular activities any activities, such as teams and clubs, that are not part of your classes

fixed spayed or neutered

marine biologist a scientist who studies plants and animals that live in or near the water

nonprofit organization a group that pays no taxes to the government in exchange for its work, which is limited to charity and community service

organizational skills the abilities you need to plan and carry out a task successfully

rehabilitate to nurse something or someone to its normal, healthy state

species a type of animal; any member of a group of animals that have the same name and characteristics

veterinarian a doctor who cures and heals sick and wounded animals

volunteer a person who does a job willingly, without payment

zoologist a scientist who studies animals

Adams, Patricia, and Jean Marzollo. *The Helping Hands Handbook: A Guidebook for Kids Who Want to Help People, Animals, and the World We Live In.* New York: Random House, 1992.

Brooks, Bruce. *Nature by Design.* New York: Farrar, Straus & Giroux, 1994.

Curtis, Patricia. *Aquatic Animals in the Wild and in Captivity.* New York: Lodestar, 1992.

Few, Roger. *MacMillan Children's Guide to Endangered Animals.* New York: Simon & Schuster, 1993.

Greenaway, Frank, and Barbara Taylor. *Look Closer: River Life. Boston*: Houghton Mifflin Co., 1992.

Lewis, Barbara A., and Pamela Espeland. *The Kid's Guide to Service Projects: Over 500 Service Ideas for Young People Who Want to Make a Difference.* Minneapolis, MN: Free Spirit Publishing, 1995

ORGANIZATIONS

Corporation for National Service:
  Learn & Serve America!
1201 New York Avenue, NW
Washington, D.C. 20525
202-606-5000
www.cns.gov

The Fund for Animals, Inc.
200 West 57th Street
New York, NY 10019
212-246-2096
Web site: *WWW.fund.org/home*
The fund works for animal causes around the
world. Check out their Web site under job
openings and internships for volunteer opportunities in your area.

The Humane Society of the United States
2100 L Street, NW
Washington, D.C. 20037
202-452-1100
Web site: *www.hsus.org*
This national office of the HSUS can direct you
to your local humane society chapter and volunteer opportunities in your region. Be sure to
check out the Project Pond on their kids' page
for great ideas about projects to help animals.

The Nature Conservancy
4245 North Fairfax Drive
Suite 100
Arlington, VA 22203-1606
800-628-6860
www.tnc.org
This site offers information on conservation
projects around the world and offers volunteer
opportunities.

About the Author

Born and raised in New York City, Claudia Isler has edited material ranging in subject from robotic engineering to soap operas. She is the author of other books for young people, including *Caught in the Middle: A Teen Guide to Custody* and *Volunteering to Help in Your Neighborhood*. She now lives with her husband in Pennsylvania, where she works as a writer and an editor.